THE MONUMENT

by Colleen Wagner

Playwrights Canada Press

Toronto • Canada

The Monument © Copyright 1993 Colleen Wagner
Playwrights Canada Press
54 Wolseley St., 2nd fl. Toronto, Ontario CANADA M5T 1A5
Tel: (416) 703-0201 Fax: (416) 703-0059
e-mail: info@puc.ca http://www.puc.ca

Playwrights Canada Press acknowledges the support of The Canada
Council for the Arts for our publishing programme
and the Ontario Arts Council.

Front cover phot by Cylla von Tiedman.
Playwright's photo by Dianne Laanamets.

Canadian Cataloguing in Publication Data
Wagner, Colleen, 1949 —
The Monument
A play
ISBN 0-88754-507-6
I. Title.
PS8595.A86M66 1996 C812'.54 C96-931229-6
PR9199.3.W35M66 1996

First edition: July, 1996. Second printing, February 1997. Third
printing, April, 2000.
Printed and bound by Hignell Printing at Winnipeg, Manitoba, Canada.

THE MONUMENT

Colleen Wagner's first play, "Sand", was selected for the final
shortlist for best international play at the Royal Exchange
Theatre in Manchester, England. Her second play, "Eclipsed",
was performed at the Words Festival, Canadian Stage
Company, Toronto. "The Monument" premiered at Canadian
Stage Company and toured to Manitoba Theatre Centre,
Winnipeg. It was also produced at Northern Light Theatre,
Edmonton and at La Mama Theatre in Melbourne, Australia. It
was nominated for a Dora Mavor Moore Award. Colleen
Wagner was born in Alberta and now lives in Toronto.

In memory of my mother,

Lucille Anne Wagner (née Caskey)

"The Monument" premiered in January, 1995 at Canadian Stage Company, Toronto, in co-production with Necessary Angel Theatre and the Manitoba Theatre Centre. It was produced in Manitoba in February, 1995 with the same cast:

MEJRA *Rosemary Dunsmore*
STETKO *Tom Barnett*

Directed by Richard Rose.
Set and costumes by Charlotte Dean.
Lighting by Kevin Lamotte.
Stage manager - Naomi Campbell.

A second performance was presented at Northern Light Theatre, Edmonton, Alberta, April 1995 with the following cast:

MEJRA *Maralyn Ryan*
STETKO *Kurt Max Runte*

Directed by D.D. Kugler.
Set and costumes by David Skelton.
Lighting by Stancil Campbell.
Sound design by Dave Clarke.
Stage manager - Susan Hayes.

The play was performed at La Mama, Melbourne, Australia, July, 1995 with the following cast:

MEJRA *Brenda Palmer*
STETKO *Bob Pavlich*

Directed by Laurence Strangio.
Set and costumes by Anna Tregloan.
Lighting by Richard Vabre.
Stage manager - Jeni Hector.

CHARACTERS

STETKO, 19   **MEJRA**, 50

Acknowledgments

There have been so many people who supported this project.
Many have already been thanked, but I wish to make special
mention of the following: Iris Turcott and Candace Burley
for nurturing this play from its first thirty pages; Don Kugler
and Richard Rose for believing in me for all those years, and
for having the courage to produce the play; Rosemary
Dunsmore and Peter Van Wart for their exceptional help and
friendship; Dave Woolacott, who has supported and
encouraged me through many creative projects and to whom
I owe a special thanks; Jane Leis and Dianna Laanamets,
who gave me a space to write and unconditional love; and
Walter Muma, for the trees.

I also want to acknowledge and thank The Canada Council,
The Ontario Arts Council, The Banff Playwrights Colony,
The New Play Development Centre at Canadian Stage
Company, Necessary Angel Theatre, and Northern Light
Theatre for their assistance in the development of the play.

I against my brother
I and my brother against our cousin
I, my brother, and cousin against the neighbour
All of us against the foreigner

Bedouin proverb

"A voice was heard in Ramah,
Sobbing and lamenting
Rachel weeping for her children,
refusing to be comforted
because they were no more."

Jeremiah 31:15

SCENE 1

STETKO is strapped to an electric chair. A single bulb above him provides the only light. He appears small in the vast darkness. He speaks to spectators sitting in a gallery behind or around him. We cannot see the gallery or the spectators.

STETKO   The one I liked the best was 17, maybe 18.
And pretty. With watery eyes.
Like a doe's.
She was like that.

I was her first.
I mean, she was a virgin.
A man can tell.
She said she wasn't, but the way she bled —
and cried —
I knew.

I didn't mean to hurt her.
Every time she cried out I pulled back.
I wanted it to last.

    Pause.

I don't care for orgasm like some men.
They only think about coming. They rush through
like they're pumping iron
just wanting to come.
Not me.
Once you come that's it.
It's over.

And there you are facing the same old things that were there before you started.

I don't care for the world much.

(*laughs*) 'Course it doesn't care much for me either.
So big deal, eh?
It don't care for me, I don't care for it...
Big deal.

The doctors — make me laugh — they're trying to figure me out.
Why I'm like this.
Nobody agrees.
Dr. Casanova — Yeah! Casanova! I think he's joking when he tells me his name. I laugh in his face.
He stares back.
He's got eyes like a chicken's.
Beady.
And small.
So I don't say nothing.
We have one-hundred and six sessions and I don't say anything. Not a word. We stare at each other for one hour, one-hundred and six times.
He thinks I'm a "passive aggressive".
I think he's fucking nuts.

They bring in another doctor.
A woman.
She comes with a body guard.
'Cause I'm dangerous.
That's what the body guard said.
"Dangerous."
I say to her, "wanna fuck?"
She says, "and then go to the forest?"
I know what she's doing — egging me on.
Trying to trick me.
Get me to talk.

I look at her and I think, this doctor has never done it
except in a nice soft bed and she doesn't do it much,
and she doesn't like it when she does do it.
She's got a tight puckered mouth.
I said to her "Is your ass like your mouth?"
She says, "No. One exhales, the other inhales. Don't
yours?"
She's funny. So I talk to her.
Except,
I don't tell her where the bodies are.

I don't remember.

   Pause.

I tell her about my girlfriend.
My girlfriend's a virgin.
She wants to do it but there's no place.
She lives at home.
Whenever we'd go into her room her mother would
listen at the door and open it all of a sudden and poke
her head in. "It's too quiet in here," she'd say. "If you
got nothing to say then you can join us in the living
room. If you do have something to say, say it and
come out here. It's not good for people to spend too
much time alone together when they've got nothing
to say." She should talk. I don't think she's said two
words to her husband since "I do" at the wedding.

We couldn't do it at my place 'cause I was in the army.
Some men would bring their girlfriends to the camp
and would do it while others watched.
I can't come when people are watching. And the men
never let you forget it when you don't come.
So I never brought my girlfriend.

I never took her to the forest.

I think she's watching.
I don't want her to think I'm nervous.

I didn't eat or drink since yesterday.
I don't want to mess my pants in front of her.

After I was arrested she went to the camps where the
women were held.
They told her that I'd been there and raped 23 girls.
At first I told her it wasn't true.
It wasn't really.
I mean I had to.
The other men forced me.
First time I said no they stripped me naked and
laughed at me — said I had no dick, said I turned into
a girl all of a sudden, that maybe they should do it to
me.

So I did it.

I couldn't come.
So they rubbed my face in shit and made me do it 'til
I came.

I faked it.

She just laid there looking at me.
She didn't care. She gave up.
She didn't even blink when I was doing it to her.
Just laid there like she was dead.

After it was over they told me to kill her.
I had to. I had lowest rank.
We took her to the forest and I shot her with my
machine gun and hid her body under a log. It'd been
raining and she was covered in mud. Somebody might
have mistaken her for a dead pig.

That was the first time I did it.
Sex.

I didn't mind killing her 'cause she knew I faked it and
I didn't want her telling anyone.

It was like that.

We went to the prison camps about every 3 days after that and would pick out women and we'd all do it then drive them out to the forest. We'd rape them again then kill them.

Everybody was doing it.
I don't know why.

That's where I saw the one I liked.
In one of the camps.
I was the first.

I got nothing against those "people" personally.
I was 17.
I had to enlist. If I didn't they'd think I was a sympathizer and they'd kill my family.
Only soldiers were getting paid.
My brothers and I were the only ones in the family making any money.
I drove a cab before but with the war nobody was taking them. Besides, only the army could buy gas.

So you do what comes up.

Who knows what that will be, eh — what life brings?
You're born.
You die.
And in between you try to live a little.

Maybe it's fate, eh? — our lives.

   Pause.

I'm not proud of what I did and I'm sorry my girlfriend found out.
I'm sorry we couldn't do it before I die.

   Pause.

I did to the one I liked what I wanted to do to my
girlfriend because I knew my girlfriend wouldn't let
me do it to her.

It was getting harder and harder to get it up.
I knew one day I'd get caught faking it.
So I took this girl to the forest after we raped her.
I got to drive alone.
The others thought I was taking her there to kill her.
I tied her up to a tree so she was just off the ground
and started talking to her.
I told her about my girlfriend, about me driving cab,
and about my uncle, who has a still out back of his
house, and how he's always dodging the authorities
and selling to them at the same time. I tell her she's
pretty
that she reminds me of my girlfriend.
My girlfriend's studying to be a nurse.
She says she wants to put some good back into the
world.

I would too.
If I knew how.
Who wouldn't, eh?
If they knew how.

    Pause.

So I take all her clothes off and she's crying and
begging me not to do it.
I want to
but I don't.
Her crying doesn't stop me.
I can't get it up.
I can't do it anymore.

That's what I really regret.
That I didn't do it with my girlfriend before I got
caught. I think I could have come with her.

The woman doctor, Nika, Dr. Nika — she wouldn't
tell me her first name — said that was reserved for
friends. Obviously I wasn't one of them.
I don't know what she told the authorities but next
thing you know I'm being tried for war crimes.
Makes me laugh.
If war is a crime why do we keep having them?
Why isn't everybody arrested?
They show us porno films and tell us doing it to
women is good for morale and they bring women in
and then after the war is over they tell us what we did
is a crime.
After it's over you find out there were rules.
Like no raping women.
(*ironic*) No massacres.
Just good clean fighting — as if it were a duel, as if it
were honourable.
As if you were brave.

Men aren't brave. We're all so scared we're going to
die we do anything to stay alive. We'll shoot a guy in
the back. We'll creep into his bedroom in the middle
of the night and shoot him in his sleep.

And we'll rape his wife and daughters.
Nobody's going to stop you.

Some of the men said we shouldn't kill the women.
We should get them all pregnant with our babies and
that's how we'd win the war.
Create a new race.

I heard some men were keeping women 'til after they
got them pregnant. Seven, eight months. Too late for
them to do anything about it.

It's a very good way to wipe out a race. Take away
their women and get them pregnant. Their own
husbands don't even want them after that. And what's

she going to do, kill her own baby and be completely alone?

They're doing it to our women too!

I never did that.

I don't care who wins the war.
It was just a job.

I guess rape is just part of it.

> *MEJRA enters. She's dressed in black and stands to STETKO's right which makes it difficult for him to see her. She looks at him impassively.*

Long, long silence.

STETKO   Are you the executioner?

No response.

I guess it's only fitting that a woman do it.

Silence.

Women can't rape men.
Too bad, eh?
There's probably a lot of women who would if they could.

Silence.

I'm as ready as I'll ever be.
I guess.

I suppose going for a piss before we begin is out of the question.

He laughs. She remains silent.

STETKO   I'm not going to say I'm sorry if that's what you're
          waiting for.
          What difference would it make?
          It won't bring them back.
          It won't undo what I did.
          It won't make me a better man.

MEJRA   Won't it?

STETKO   Ah, she has a tongue.

              Pause. He strains to see her.

          (*derisive*) I'm sorry.
          Feel better?

MEJRA   Should I?

STETKO   Isn't that what forgiveness is all about?
          I say sorry and the world forgives me.

          I'M SORRY.

              Silence.

          I don't mean it, of course, and so how can I expect
          forgiveness.

MEJRA   Is that what you want?

STETKO   I want to do it with my girlfriend.
          And I want to take a leak.
          My life is simple.

MEJRA   So take a leak.

          Do you think we haven't seen a man pee his pants
          before?

MEJRA	If you were a dog you could pee down your leg quite easily. But you're not a dog are you? And so you can't pee your own pants. You're too dignified for that. You may think other people act like animals but not you. You're a good person. A good dog, who has only had a bad owner.
STETKO	Are you a doctor?
MEJRA	No.
STETKO	Missionary?
MEJRA	No.
STETKO	A mother?
MEJRA	...no.
	Silence.
STETKO	And you're not the executioner...?
MEJRA	I'm your savior.
STETKO	Oh yeah?
MEJRA	Yes.
STETKO	Maybe I don't want to be saved.
MEJRA	That's up to you.
STETKO	What do you mean?
MEJRA	I can have you released.
STETKO	Is this a joke?

MEJRA   No joke.

STETKO   You can set me free?!

MEJRA   On condition.

STETKO   What condition?

MEJRA   You must do as I say for the rest of your life.

STETKO   Do as — just do whatever you say?

MEJRA   Yes.

STETKO   Like...anything?

MEJRA   Everything.

STETKO   No deal.

MEJRA   As you wish. (*begins to exit*)

STETKO   Wait!
               What if you asked me to kill myself?

MEJRA   Then you would have to do it.

               Silence.

STETKO   Would you?
               Is that it? The State's too bankrupt to do it? It's a new
               way to save money — get the prisoners to do it
               themselves.
               That's it, isn't it?
               They're too cheap.
               Maybe the power's been cut off, eh.
               What a laugh!

               Silence.

MEJRA   It's up to you.

STETKO   What kind of choice is that?

MEJRA   The only one you have.

STETKO   One choice is no choice.

MEJRA   You have two.

STETKO   I do it or they do it.

MEJRA   They do it or you obey me for the rest of your life.

               Silence.

STETKO   Why would they do that?

MEJRA   If you want to find out you'll have to postpone your
           death.

STETKO   What if I don't do as you tell me?

MEJRA   What do you think — that you'll get away with it?
           Run and hide
           — like a frightened dog?

           Where can you go?
           Everyone knows your face.

           You're the most hated man in the world.

STETKO   Is that true?

MEJRA   What do you think?
           You kill twenty-three young girls and people will
           love you for it?

STETKO   So why do you want to save me?

MEJRA   You'll have to agree to the conditions if you want to
              find out.

              (*checking her watch*) It's time.

                    STETKO experiences a few frantic moments.
                    MEJRA begins to leave.

STETKO   Sure!
              Okay.
              What have I got to lose.

                    Lights out.

                          ***

SCENE 2

That night. STETKO fingers the last morsels of food from a bowl and sucks his fingers clean.

STETKO   (*after a satisfying burp*) Very good.
Prison food is the worst.
Sometimes I wouldn't eat it.
I left some in a corner once. Even the rats wouldn't touch it.
But today I might have.

MEJRA   Freedom makes everything look good?

STETKO   Even makes you and your scowling face look good.

So, you live here?

MEJRA   Yes.

STETKO   No husband about?

MEJRA   Killed.

STETKO   I lost a brother.
And sister.
Do you have any beer?

MEJRA   Yes, but none of it is for you.

STETKO   Aah. I see.

MEJRA   What do you see?

STETKO   Nothing.

MEJRA   Then why do you say "I see" when you in fact see
          nothing?

STETKO   It's just a phrase.

MEJRA   It's also a lie.

STETKO   Truth. Lie. What difference does it make?

MEJRA   Don't you know?

          Pause.

STETKO   What do you want me to say?

MEJRA   Tell the truth.

STETKO   Everybody said what I did was wrong. That I should
          die for what I did. Bad people are punished. Isn't that
          the truth? Bad people go to jail.
          Good people, innocent people go free.
          I'm free.
          So tell me, am I bad or good?
          What's the truth?

MEJRA   You're not free.

STETKO   From my shoes, things look different.

          *MEJRA swiftly picks up a small farm sickle
          which has been stuck in the ground, and with a
          single smooth motion deliberately slices off his
          ear. As he falls to the ground she clamps a collar
          and chain around his neck and fastens it to a bolt
          in the ground. He gasps for air.*

MEJRA   Get up.

> *She kicks him sharply. He cries and gasps on the ground.*

MEJRA   Get up!

> *He rises slowly, realizing, as he rises, that he is bound.*

STETKO   What is this —?!

> *She strikes him across the face and chest.*

What are you doing!?

> *She slaps his mouth.*

MEJRA   (*ordering*) You will be silent.

STETKO   Why are you doing this?

> *She strikes his mouth again.*

MEJRA   You will be silent.

> *STETKO goes to speak but thinks better of it.*
>
> *MEJRA begins to beat him, methodically, dispassionately, one open-handed slap after another.*
>
> *STETKO rages, straining to fight back.*

STETKO   STOP IT!

> *She stops.*

MEJRA   You will be silent and you will take your beating like a man.

STETKO   Why should I?

MEJRA   Because that's the deal.

STETKO   Are you going to beat me to death?

MEJRA   I am going to beat you until you fall to the ground or
until I'm unable to beat you any longer.

> *She strikes him and STETKO immediately falls.*

Get up.

STETKO   I've fallen.

MEJRA   Get up you coward.

> *Pause.*

Last time.

> *STETKO reluctantly, but obediently, rises.*

Stand up tall.

> *He leans into the collar and prepares himself for
> the beating. MEJRA stands in front of him and
> begins the beating, a beating which seems to last
> forever.*
>
> *The lighting changes to indicate a passing of
> time into night and a slivered moon. In this light
> we only see her back and her arms swinging back
> and forth as she strikes him.*
>
> *MEJRA stops for a breath.*

MEJRA   Get down.

*He goes to his knees, shakily. She takes off a
scarf and bandages his ear. They both fight back
tears.*

STETKO   Why did you do that?

MEJRA   Because you don't know the difference between the
truth and a lie.

STETKO   I don't even know you.
Do I?
Have we ever met?
Have I — have I ever done anything to you?

MEJRA   You don't know me.
We've never met before.
(*finishing the bandaging*) Not like a nurse would do
it, not like your girlfriend, but it will serve its
purpose.

STETKO   Do you know my girlfriend?

MEJRA   I know of her.

STETKO   Because of me?

MEJRA   Of course.

STETKO   She was there, wasn't she?
At the jail?
She must know I'm here.
I'd like to see her.
...can I?

MEJRA   She's dead.

Silence.

STETKO   I know she was there.

MEJRA   You saw her?

STETKO   She said she'd come.
She said she'd see if she could come in with me —
near the end.

MEJRA   She was shot on her way to the jail.

STETKO   (*on his feet*) You're lying!

MEJRA   If that's what you choose to believe.

STETKO   Tell me you're lying!

MEJRA   I'm lying.

Silence.

STETKO   Is it true?

MEJRA   Don't you know?

STETKO   (*stunned*) Is she really dead?

MEJRA   You tell me.

STETKO   Show me proof!
The police report!

MEJRA   Why should I?
Why should I tell you, prove to *you*?
Who are you to ask for anything?

STETKO   I have a right to know the truth!

Long silence.

STETKO	She's alive.
	I know it.
	You're playing games with my mind.
	I know about mind games.
MEJRA	Time for bed.
	You sleep out here.
STETKO	Outside?
MEJRA	Outside.

She exits. He stands stubbornly.

STETKO	Fuck you.
	Fuck you.

Blackout.

***

SCENE 3

STETKO, shackled, is yoked to a wooden plough.
MEJRA is behind guiding it. The plow is stuck.

MEJRA   Can't you pull harder, Stinko?

STETKO   It's Stetko.
Stet-ko.

MEJRA   I prefer Stinko.

STETKO   I prefer not to pull harder.

MEJRA   You have no say in the matter.

> *Silence.*
> *He leans into the yoke.*

STETKO   It won't budge.

MEJRA   If we can't make something of this land we'll starve.

> *They look at the charred ruins of the land.*

STETKO   Sometimes I think we should all starve.
We'd be better off.

MEJRA   (*laughing*) Stinko, you are so stupid you're funny.

STETKO   Don't call me Stinko okay?
Please.

> *Pause.*

MEJRA   Okay.

             Silence.

             He tries again. It won't budge.

STETKO   Maybe nothing will grow anyway.
             It's probably been poisoned.
             We sometimes sprayed.

MEJRA   There are landmines also.

STETKO   Here?!

MEJRA   Afraid to die?

STETKO   Everybody is afraid to die.

MEJRA   Is that so?

STETKO   Sure.
             Except when living looks worse. Then they want to die.

MEJRA   Were the women you killed like that?

STETKO   Some.

MEJRA   All?

STETKO   Some.

MEJRA   Who?

STETKO   I don't remember.

MEJRA   What were their names?

STETKO   I don't know.
             Why?

Silence.

MEJRA   Pull.

STETKO   It won't budge.

MEJRA   We have to dig it out.

STETKO   (*in the yoke*) How can I?

> *Long silence.*

> *STETKO grins. MEJRA begins to dig with her hands. STETKO leans against the plough and whistles a light tune. MEJRA, angry, digs harder, faster.*

STETKO   (*looking up*) Sunstroke weather.

> *She looks up at him in anger. He grins back.*

Take off the yoke, Mejra.

> *She resumes digging.*

I've met people like you before.
Stubborn.
So stubborn they don't know when they're beat.
When they need the help of others. Even if they don't like those others.

MEJRA   This rock was never here before!

STETKO   Maybe it's not a rock.
Maybe it is a landmine.

> *MEJRA weeps.*

Hey, it's a joke.
It's a rock.

STETKO   It's obvious it's a rock. I'm joking.

                You have to laugh at life sometimes.
                Otherwise you go mad.

MEJRA   That's your remedy is it?

STETKO   (*shrugs*) Got a better idea?

                MEJRA swiftly unhooks him from the yoke,
                cuffs his hands in front, and drags him by his
                chains to the rock.

MEJRA   Dig it out.

STETKO   How?

MEJRA   With your feet. Your mouth. Your nose.
                I don't care.
                Just do it.

                STETKO assesses the rock for a moment then
                proceeds to poke with one foot. He whistles a
                long note.

STETKO   She's a big one.

MEJRA   Dig.

                He works harder, using both feet. This motion
                develops into a kind of Russian jig or march. He
                sings and kicks at the dirt until he tires.

STETKO   This is sunstroke weather.

MEJRA   For idiots, yes.

STETKO   What's life, eh?
                Drudgery, and a few dances in between.
                Care to dance, madam?

MEJRA   Dig.

STETKO   Take off my shirt.

                It's hot.

                I like the sun.
                I never saw daylight in prison.
                It's the first hot day of the year.

                MEJRA strikes him

MEJRA   Stinko, you are nothing.
                No one.
                A dog.
                A slave.
                A murderer.

STETKO   I know what I am.
                I know I'm a murderer
                and a dog
                and a slave.
                I don't care.
                I'm not proud.
                I can be those things.

MEJRA   You *are* those things.

STETKO   So what?
                So what do we do with that?
                Kill me?
                You went to a lot of trouble to save me.
                Why? Eh?
                What do you want?
                I'm your dog and slave.
                I'm Stinko the murderer.
                So what?

                She sits on the rock.

MEJRA	So what. Right. So what. What do we do with dogs and slaves and murderers. What would you do?
STETKO	Shoot them probably.
MEJRA	Shoot them.
STETKO	Yeah. It's simple.
MEJRA	Maybe I should shoot you.
STETKO	You like me.
MEJRA	Understand one thing if you can stupido — I despise you.
STETKO	So shoot me.

> *Silence.*

STETKO	So use me like a dog and a slave 'til it's time to shoot me. Do you think I care. Eh? What do I have to care about?
MEJRA	Don't look for pity! Dig!

> *Pause.*

> *He begins, furious at first, then grins and switches again to his manic dance, singing at the top of his lungs, kicking dirt everywhere until the rock is exposed. He clasps his handcuffed arms around the boulder and heaves with all his*

might and lifts the rock triumphantly to his chest. He turns as if he would hurl the rock at her, but it's impossible.

MEJRA   Go ahead.
Show me what you're really made of.
Smash my face with it.

STETKO laughs at his own impotence.

Drop it on your foot.

STETKO   (*suddenly serious*) I can't.

MEJRA   Why not?

STETKO   I don't know.

MEJRA puts her foot beneath the rock.

MEJRA   Drop it on mine.

He releases the rock immediately. She pulls her foot away in time.

Try again.

STETKO   (*laughs*) It's too heavy.

MEJRA   Pick it up.

STETKO   You are one strange woman.

MEJRA   Who are you to judge?
Pick it up.

STETKO attempts to pick it up but can't.

STETKO   Impossible.

MEJRA	A moment ago it was possible. Pick it up or I'll bury you in this field.
STETKO	I can't pick it up now. I had strength then. I don't now. I used it all up. Who do you think I am — Hercules? I can lift mountains on command?
MEJRA	Didn't you kill on command?

       No response.

       Which is harder? Killing someone or lifting a
mountain?
Is that where your strength is Stinko?
In hatred?
If you hate enough you can lift a mountain and kill a
people, on command.

STETKO	I don't hate them.
MEJRA	You kill people you like?

       Silence.

       Learn to hate me Stinko, because you are going to lift
that rock on command or be buried alive in this field.

STETKO	I wish you'd never come to save me.
MEJRA	I never came to save you.
STETKO	You said you were my savior.

MEJRA   I lied.

                 You know all about lies don't you?
                 Haven't you ever said to a young girl, I'll show you
                 the forest.

STETKO   I never!

MEJRA   Someday you'll take me to this forest.

STETKO   What do you mean?

MEJRA   You look nervous.
                 We all know about the forest.
                 Dead bodies.
                 Not your girlfriend though.
                 She died on the street.
                 A virgin.

                 STETKO weeps.

                 You're right, Stetko.
                 I am your savior.

                 Now pick up that rock because you owe me.
                 Pick it up out of gratitude instead of hate.

                 Go on.

                 He tries, but in vain.

                 Hate works best for you.

STETKO   For you too.
                 You hate me.

MEJRA   Yes.

STETKO   Why?

MEJRA   I might kill you before I could finish my sentence.

     Pause.

STETKO   You're one of "them", aren't you?

MEJRA   What if I am?

STETKO   My aunt is one.
My father's brother married one.
I used to see them a lot.
Before.

Now everybody fights.
The whole family.

Everyone thinks they're right.
That's why people need someone to take charge.
Keep people in line. Make them shut up and do as
they're told.

MEJRA   You?

STETKO   Not me
but somebody.

MEJRA   Then you'll like our arrangement.
It's a dictatorship.
I'm the dictator.
I tell you what to do and you do it.

STETKO   Sure.
I don't care.
People don't care who's in charge just so long as they
don't have to take responsibility.

MEJRA   I'll take responsibility.
Pick up the rock and drop it on your foot.

STETKO   It's not normal to injure yourself.

MEJRA   It's normal to harm someone else?

STETKO   I've done nothing to you.

MEJRA   (*suddenly angry*) Pick up the rock.

STETKO   I can't.

           He grins.

           Funny thing about "dictators" eh?
           What happens when nobody does as they're told?
           What's the dictator to do? Kill them all?
           Then there'd be nobody left to do all the dirty work.
           Then the dictator isn't a dictator anymore.
           Maybe everybody is pretending to be who they are.
           Maybe everybody has to believe a lie.

MEJRA   And what lie do you want to believe — that I'm here
           to save you, or to bury you alive?

STETKO   (*grins*) I believe you like me.
           But you're too old and ugly for a young guy like me.

MEJRA   Too ugly to be raped, too old to be impregnated.
           Just right for killing.

STETKO   For sure. We would have just shot you.

MEJRA   I would have considered myself lucky.

STETKO   Strange world, eh?

MEJRA   What will it be?
           Choose.

           Pause.

           Pick it up.

STETKO   No.

               Pause.

               MEJRA starts digging STETKO's grave with her
               hands

               What are you doing?

MEJRA   Guess.

STETKO   You stupid bitch fucking cunt —

               He heaves the rock to his chest

MEJRA   (*slaps him across the face*) Don't ever call me that
               again.

STETKO   What's with you?
               I lift it.
               I drop it.
               Doesn't matter what I do I get slapped down.
               You wouldn't touch me if I wasn't tied up.

MEJRA   You wouldn't rape girls if they were armed.

STETKO   (*laughs*) Guess not.
               You think I'm stupid?
               I know they don't like it.

MEJRA   No they don't.

STETKO   You been raped?

MEJRA   None of your business.

STETKO   I take that for yes.

MEJRA   I don't care how you take it, just understand this, the
               military is not the only one with power.

STETKO	(*grins*) Untie me, Mejra.
MEJRA	(*grins back*) Not yet, Stinko.
STETKO	This rock is too fucking heavy.
MEJRA	Drop it — except on your foot — and I bury you alive.
STETKO	What is the point of this?
MEJRA	The right to choose.
STETKO	Hold it, break my foot, or be buried alive?!
MEJRA	I knew you had some potential, Stinko.

> *She exits.*

STETKO	Don't call me Stinko! It's Stetko. Stet-ko Tef-te-dar-i-ja. Stupid —

> *He stops short just in case she hears him. He holds the rock as the lights indicate the coming of night. He sings a marching tune, baldly, defiantly.*

> *Blackout.*

***

SCENE 4

MEJRA is bandaging STETKO's foot. He shivers from cold and shock.

MEJRA   Papa cut his tail off and he howled and wailed through the night and in the morning the poison was out of his system.
The shock drove it out of his body.
He was my father's favorite dog.
He used to say "I loved that dog enough to chop its tail off — which is more than I could do for my children."

STETKO   What if he had died?

MEJRA   Who knows.
We only ever know what does happen.

STETKO   I wouldn't have done that.
I probably would have just watched, to see if he'd make it on his own.
See if he was meant to live.

MEJRA   Who decides that?
Who decides who will live and who won't?

STETKO   (*shrugs*) I don't know.

MEJRA   My father loved that dog.

STETKO   (*grins*) Like you love me?

MEJRA   I don't love you.

STETKO   You sure?

MEJRA   Positive.

STETKO   You live out here alone.
No neighbours.
Nothing.
You see me. Young —

MEJRA   (*bursts out laughing*) You are so arrogant and stupid
—
I think all your brains must be in your cock.
And you're impotent!

STETKO   Not anymore.
Last night I had a hard on.
That's why I dropped the rock.
So I could masturbate.

MEJRA   You lie.

                    Pause.

STETKO   Yeah.
I couldn't hold it any longer.
My back was killing me.
In a way I was relieved when it fell.

MEJRA   Nothing like pain to stop...everything.

I have something for you.

STETKO   A gift?

MEJRA   Sort of.
I found it.

STETKO   What is it?

MEJRA

A rabbit.
It had been caught in a snare and chewed its front paw
off to escape.
I was going to kill it for dinner but it snarled at me.
I thought anything that wants to live that badly
deserves a chance. So I brought it home.

STETKO

I had a pet rabbit when I was seven.
Where is it?

MEJRA

There, in the basket.

> *STETKO limps to the basket, opens it, and
> looks in*

STETKO

It hissed at me!

MEJRA

Maybe it doesn't want our help.
Maybe it wants to die.

STETKO

Nobody wants to die.

MEJRA

How do you know?

STETKO

...I saw lots of people die.

MEJRA

The girls?

STETKO

Yeah. Some of them didn't seem to care.
But they probably knew it was for the best. Nobody
wants a woman who's been raped.
Husbands walk away.

MEJRA

Mothers never walk away.

> *Silence. STETKO considers this statement.*

That's where men always become confused.
They don't know what to do about mothers.

STETKO   It bit me!

           He sucks his finger and closes the basket.

           Look at me.
           No ear.
           Crushed foot.
           Bit finger.

MEJRA   Should we kill it?

STETKO   — no.

MEJRA   Why not?

STETKO   It doesn't know any different.
           It doesn't know I'm a friend.

           What are you smiling about?

MEJRA   I'm not. I'm musing.
           We forgive an animal but not a people.

           Well, it's yours then.

           She gives him dinner.

           This is all there is.

STETKO   What is this?

MEJRA   It was growing near the marsh.

STETKO   A man can't live on this.

MEJRA   Eat the rabbit then. That's all there is.

           She exits.

STETKO   And what did you have, eh?!
                Beer?
                Potatoes with gravy?
                Some cabbage?
                Stewed beef and cabbage with potatoes and paprika,
                and carrots.
                Dumplings.
                I'll die on this!
                She's going to starve me to death.

                    *The rabbit scratches at the basket. He opens it
                    and looks in.*

                Where do you think you're going, eh? With 3 feet.
                What a pair.
                Maybe if we team up we'll have enough feet between
                us to escape.

                Maybe I ought to eat you instead.
                Stay and eat — run and —
                and what?
                Be eaten?
                What a life, eh?
                Eat or be eaten.
                What a fucking life.
                That's it though, isn't it.
                At least for you.
                I'm a man.
                I'm supposed to be above that.

                (*starting to eat*) But I'm not.

                    He shares some of his greens with the rabbit.

                I'm not.

                    Blackout.

                            ✳✳✳

SCENE 5

STETKO is bent over looking closely at a small green growth in the plowed field. The rabbit is beside him in the basket. He straightens up suddenly and runs, still shackled, as far as the chain leash permits.

STETKO MEJRAA!
Something is growing!

He runs back to the growth and examines it further.

A green thing.
What though?
It's not even in the row.
Maybe it's a weed.
(*grins*) Maybe it's — rabbit food!
That's what you wish, eh?
Is that what you wish?
A big green salad?
Even if it's a weed?
MEJRAAAA.

It must be a weed.
Nothing else is growing except it.
Do you like weeds, eh?
Would you like to try a leaf or two?

STETKO plucks a leaf but the whole plant comes up.

STETKO   Oh shit! The whole thing's come up.
                Maybe it was dying anyway.
                What do you think?
                A plant comes up that easy — can't be meant to live,
                eh?

                He dangles it over the opened basket.

                Feast your eyes on that.
                Do you want it?
                Roll over.
                (*laughs*) You're no dummy.
                Only dogs roll over for their dinner.
                And play dead.
                Because you're so smart you can have it.
                Don't bite my fingers.
                Gently.
                You see, even a stupid animal can learn.
                Yes, you'll let me pet you as long as I feed you.
                It's nice, eh?
                Feels good.

                MEJRA enters with cut flowers.

MEJRA   Look what I found.
                Growing.
                Wild flowers.

STETKO   They're nice.
                Pretty.

MEJRA   They're weeds really but who names the rose?

STETKO   Huh?

MEJRA   Never mind.
                Why were you shouting?

STETKO   Something was growing here too.

MEJRA
Of course.
I planted it this morning.
It's a wild bean plant.
I found it by the marsh.
A lone survivor.

STETKO
Lone?
The only one?

MEJRA
I don't know how it grew, but there it was, so I
uprooted it and brought it here.

STETKO
I don't think it will make it.

MEJRA
Why not?

STETKO
Too hot.

MEJRA
It's not too hot.

STETKO
Too dry.

MEJRA
We'll carry water from the mountains if we have to.
It'll grow.
It has to.
That's all there is.

What's the matter?

What have you done, Stinko?
You look — ridiculous.

She pushes him aside and can't see the plant.

Where is it!?

Did you eat it, you pig?!

STETKO
No.

MEJRA   Did you feed it to that damn rabbit!

STETKO   No.

MEJRA   Then where is it?

           STETKO shrugs and looks confused.

           Don't you realize that was our chance to grow something?!

STETKO   I'll do without.

MEJRA   You idiot!
           We'll all do without!

           She sees the rabbit.

MEJRA   You fed it to the rabbit.
           (*snatching it*) Give me that.

           It is a gnawed nub.

           Nothing.
           Chewed the vital part first.

           She strikes STETKO.

           Shit for brains.

STETKO   I thought it was a weed.

MEJRA   It was!
           One we could eat.

STETKO   We'll find something else.

MEJRA   What?

STETKO — flowers.
Mix them with something.
Grass!
Roast them.

MEJRA I can't believe you!

STETKO I didn't know!
I wouldn't have done it if I'd known.
Why didn't you tell me?

MEJRA I don't have to report to you.

STETKO No, but if you'd told me — if you'd said
"Hey, Stinko, I planted a wild bean in the field, don't
feed it to the rabbit — "

> *She realizes his attachment to the rabbit and
> makes a step toward it.*

MEJRA Give me the rabbit.

STETKO (*steps between it and her*) No.

MEJRA Get out of my way.

STETKO — no.

MEJRA Move, or I'll beat you purple.

STETKO Please, Mejra.
She's mine.

MEJRA She's not yours any more than the sun is yours.
The air
the water
this land.
You own nothing!

STETKO Then why did you give her to me?

MEJRA   I heard something about your girlfriend.
                 She was raped.

STETKO   You lie!

MEJRA   She was shot first.
                 Killed.
                 Then raped.
                 She was lucky, wouldn't you say?
                 She didn't have to endure the — what —
                 indignity?
                 Pain?
                 A lucky girl.

STETKO   You lie.

MEJRA   Yes. I lie.
                 We all lie.
                 Why do we do that, Stetko?
                 Why do you lie?

STETKO   I don't know.

MEJRA   Think!

STETKO   Depends on the lie.

MEJRA   You lied about the rabbit.
                 You said she didn't eat the green.
                 Why?

STETKO   I was afraid you'd hurt her.

MEJRA   Do you think the first lie ever told was to protect
                 another?

STETKO   ...maybe.

MEJRA   You think we're that noble?

STETKO   Probably the first person to tell a lie did it to save himself.

MEJRA   From what?
What are we saving ourselves from?

STETKO   I don't know.

MEJRA   Think!
What are you afraid of Stetko?

Silence.

STETKO   What do you want to hear?
I'll say anything.
I don't care.
Whatever you want.
Do you think just because somebody says something they mean it?

MEJRA   You lie to make life easier for yourself?
It's more convenient to go along with the others?

STETKO   Sure.

MEJRA   You raped and killed girls because it was easier than disobeying orders.

STETKO   Yes!
Yesyesyes!
It's easier to obey.
I obey authority.
I obey you.
It's easier.

MEJRA   I guess that's why the soldiers killed your girlfriend first.
It's easier to rape them when they're dead.

STETKO   She wasn't raped!

MEJRA   Yes she was.
Gang raped.
From the back.

He covers his ears and sings wildly fighting tears.
MEJRA exits.

Lights indicate night and a lambent moon.
STETKO stops singing and sobs.

Lights out.

***

SCENE 6

The same lambent moon. MEJRA enters with a jar. STETKO stands defeated.

MEJRA
I brought you a beer.

He looks at it, at her, then takes it.

STETKO
(*ironic, toasting*) To life. (*and swallows a large mouthful*)
It's warm.

MEJRA
Yes.

STETKO
Who cares, eh?
To life!

He drinks.

MEJRA
To life.
To children.
To love.

STETKO
To love.
Who knows about love.

MEJRA
I do.

STETKO
You are the cruellest woman I know.

MEJRA
Kindness is not love.
Besides, I don't love you.

STETKO   You hate me.

MEJRA   Yes.

STETKO   Why do you hate me so much?

                    Silence.

                    Why did you bring me here?

MEJRA   Drink up Stetko.

STETKO   Thank you.
                    For not calling me Stinko.

                    Is it late?

MEJRA   Almost morning.

STETKO   You couldn't sleep.

MEJRA   No.

STETKO   Me either.

MEJRA   I know.

STETKO   You watch me?

MEJRA   I just know.

STETKO   Was she really raped?
                    Tell me the truth Mejra.

MEJRA   What is the truth?
                    I tell you your girlfriend is dead.
                    Raped.
                    I can't show you the body.
                    There is no body to be found.

MEJRA   People tell you one thing.
                   The military tells another.

                   We'll read about the war in the papers — new
                   territories divided among the victors.
                   New leaders.
                   Economic decisions determined by outside interests.
                   There will be medals for the dead soldiers on all sides.
                   Plaques for the brave and foolhearty.
                   Monuments for the Generals.

                   What will anyone know about you and your
                   girlfriend?
                   About me?
                   About the girls in the forest?

                   What is the truth?

                   The truth
                   is like love.
                   It defies words.
                   It's known without "facts".

STETKO   Was she or wasn't she?

MEJRA   She's missing.
                   That's all we know.
                   That's the "facts."
                   Now, what is the truth?
                   You're a soldier. You know how a soldier's mind
                   works.
                   Is she alive?
                   A virgin?

STETKO   Maybe she's hiding.

MEJRA   Yes, maybe she's hiding.

                   Silence.

STETKO   Things happen in war.
              We're trained to follow orders. Our lives depend on it.
              It's automatic.
              Soldiers aren't supposed to think.
              Only obey.

MEJRA   I guess you'll bear the "other side" no ill will if
              they've captured your girlfriend.

                      STETKO drinks.

STETKO   Warm beer is better than no beer.

MEJRA   (*ironic*)
              "Facts" are better than truth.
              Revenge is better than sorrow.

STETKO   I hope I never grow old and bitter like you.

MEJRA   Then chances are you'll die young.

STETKO   (*shrugs*) What can I do?
              I'm a prisoner.
              I do nothing.
              I think nothing.

MEJRA   Right.
              You're helpless.
              I'm helpless.
              We're all victims of fate.

                      *She can see STETKO thinking about the issue of
                      fate.*

              Is war fate?

STETKO   I don't know.

MEJRA   And the girls?

STETKO   (*shrugs*) A girl walks by
and —
In a war
you can get away with it.

Everybody's doing it.
Rape is just part of war.

That's how some men pump themselves up.
Get their adrenaline going.
Makes them reckless.
Fearless.
I've seen men run into the open afterwards, spraying
bullets.
Most of them get shot down, but some don't and they
come back looking like heroes.
Everyone cheers.
They get first pick of the women.

I never did it.
Run in the open.

MEJRA   You only shot women.

STETKO   Yeah.
That's how it was.

        He drinks.

That was their fate.

MEJRA   They cut her tongue out
and slit her open from her vagina to her navel
and filled the hole with dirt
and pissed on it.

STETKO   I don't believe you anymore.

MEJRA   That's right.
We all know soldiers don't do that to women and
children.
Men don't do that sort of thing.
We all know that.
Isn't that the "truth"?

Tomorrow we go to the forest.

She exits.

A pale light of dawn.

Blackout.

***

SCENE 7

They stand in the forest.

STETKO   It's gone.

MEJRA   She.
She is not an it.

STETKO   She.
She's gone.
Animals must have got her.

MEJRA   This was the first one you killed?

STETKO   Yeah.

MEJRA   Where's the log? You said you put a log over her
body.

STETKO   Someone must have taken it for firewood.

MEJRA   No evidence.

STETKO   No.

MEJRA   No one is going to know the truth.
That's the plan isn't it?
Keep it secret.
No reminders.

Maybe you're lying.
Maybe this isn't the right place.

STETKO   This is the right place.

                    Silence.

MEJRA   Do you know her name?

STETKO   I didn't ask.

MEJRA   Missing.
                    That's her epitaph.
                    Missing.

                    Where are the others?

STETKO   I don't know.

MEJRA   You knew where she was, where are the others?

STETKO   I don't know.
                    This was the first one I killed.
                    The first always sticks in the mind.
                    After that it was —
                    I don't know —

MEJRA   Routine?

STETKO   Sort of.

MEJRA   What about the girl you liked the best?
                    The virgin.
                    What was her name?

STETKO   I don't know.

MEJRA   Think!

STETKO   I don't remember.

MEJRA   You don't remember or *won't* remember?

STETKO   I *don't* remember.

Silence.

MEJRA   Where is she?

Pause.

STETKO   A different place.

MEJRA   Where?

STETKO   In a grave.

MEJRA   You buried her?

STETKO   We dug a big grave and put lots of them in it.

MEJRA   Where is it?

STETKO   I don't remember!

MEJRA   Take me there.

STETKO   How can I when I don't know where it is?!

MEJRA   What will make you remember?

STETKO   What?

MEJRA   What do I have to do to you to make you remember?

STETKO   Some things are just gone from memory.
Blocked out.

MEJRA   (*hands him a shovel*) Start digging.

STETKO   It's not here!

MEJRA   Your own grave.
               Start digging.

STETKO   Things have changed!
               The markings are different.
               Trees have been cut
               and —
               (*looking up, remembering*)
               It was west
               the sun was in my eyes
               it was late afternoon.

MEJRA   Find it.

STETKO   There was a tree
               a large tree
               there were bullet holes in the bark
               and a strong branch hung low —
               the one I tied her up to.
               I see it
               but I don't know where it is now.

MEJRA   Then dig.

STETKO   I'm not sure where it is!

MEJRA   Then dig!

STETKO   Come on, Mejra.

MEJRA   (*strikes him*) Find her.

               Pause.

               *STETKO wanders in one direction, stops, shakes
               his head and then wanders in another direction.*

STETKO   No.

He wanders, thinks he's getting close, stops, uncertain. He takes a few steps further. MEJRA stands impassive and watches.

Meanwhile, the lighting has gradually changed to indicate the passing of time and a change of location. They are now deeper in the forest; it is darker, the shadows are longer.

STETKO stops and looks down.

STETKO   This is it.

MEJRA comes to the spot.

MEJRA   Here?

STETKO   Yes.

MEJRA   Are you sure?

STETKO   I'm sure.

MEJRA   How do you know?

STETKO   I can tell.
I can feel it.

MEJRA   Feel what?

STETKO   I don't know.

STETKO remembers.

MEJRA   Tell me.

Silence.

MEJRA   Tell me, Stetko.
            They mustn't be forgotten.
            Same as your girlfriend.
            They must not be forgotten.

                Pause.

            You liked her the best.

            Tell me.

                Pause.

STETKO   I was driving the jeep.
            I was laughing.
            Finally I was alone.
            I got to drive on my own — with her,
            this girl.
            I felt really good.
            The sun was shining the whole time.
            I was singing
            I'm finally alone with this girl.
            And I'm singing —

                He sings a popular song.

            I look over at her
            and she's not smiling
            just looking straight ahead.
            I'd forgot you see,
            I forgot what I was supposed to be doing —
            killing them.
            I forgot.
            I was suddenly a free man going for a ride with my
            girl.

            Then everything got serious.
            I don't remember anything until we get here
            and I tell her to lift her arms up over her head.
            And she does.

I tie her hands together and throw the rope over the
tree branch.
It's gone now.
Somebody has cut it down.

I pull the rope 'til she's stretched as far as she can go
and then I pull 'til she's just off the ground.
She looks so pretty.
Big watery eyes
like a doe's.
I cut her dress —
because her hands are tied and I can't get it off
otherwise.
I use my hunting knife.
She's got very white skin.
It's never seen the sun.
She's got a thin line of black hairs that run up to her
belly button.
I think it's quite sexy.
I tell her so.
I go up to her
and
put my arms around her
and kiss her neck.
I figure I can do it with her.
I feel her shiver.
I ask her if she's cold.
She says "no".
I ask her if she's afraid.
She shakes her head
but I think she's lying.
I ask her if she wants me to undress —
maybe she hasn't seen a man before
naked.
She closes her eyes
tight.
So I tell her I won't take my clothes off
and she opens them again
and I can see she's crying.

So I stop
and sit down on a log
or rock
and I tell her about myself
and my uncle.
I tell her about my girlfriend.

I ask her what she wants to be when she grows up.
She says she wants to be a teacher.
I tell her she's just like my girlfriend
wanting to put some good back into the world.
I tell her I would too
if I knew how.

I tell her she's beautiful.
I tell her I want to do it with her.

I figure maybe I can come with her.

She begs me not to
but I try anyway.

Only I can't.
I can't get hard.
It won't go in.
I can't do it anymore.

It's all over.

> *Pause.*

I don't know what to do.

She begs me to set her free.
And I'm thinking "what if I do?"
What if I set her free. What will happen?
I'm scared — in case the others find out —
they'd kill me for letting the enemy go.

She says she won't tell anyone.
I notice her hands are swollen and white.
It's getting late
the sun's going down
I have to return the jeep.

So I leave it to fate.
I say, "Let's see if she's meant to live."

I back away
and
close my eyes
and aim the gun
and I say to myself
if I miss,
no matter what,
I let her go.

     Pause.

It hit her in the face.

     Silence.

I cut her down and dragged her to a grave we'd dug
before but hadn't covered over
and I put her into it
and buried her.

     Long, long silence.

MEJRA   Dig it open.

STETKO   What!?

MEJRA   Dig the grave open.

STETKO   She's dead!

MEJRA   Dig it open!

STETKO   I can't.
I'll be sick.

MEJRA   Be sick, but dig.

STETKO   What's the point!

MEJRA   Proof.
We want the "facts".

STETKO   I did it like I said!

MEJRA   Stetko you will dig open that grave or you will dig
your own and lie in it.
Choose.

        Pause.

        STETKO takes the shovel and digs.

STETKO   It's been a while.
There might not be anything left.

MEJRA   Dig.

        He digs.

STETKO   I hear corpses carry diseases.

MEJRA   None worse than any the living carry.

        He digs deeper.

STETKO   Maybe this is the wrong spot.

MEJRA   It'll be the right one for you.

        He digs even deeper.

STETKO   There were a lot of bodies.
           How will I know which is her?

MEJRA   Because her spirit will return and shriek her name.

           He drops the shovel and scrambles out. MEJRA
           blocks his way.

           Afraid of spirits?

STETKO   We shouldn't be doing this!

MEJRA   Why?
           Afraid to revisit?
           Do you feel graves are haunted —
           that the spirits of the dead linger on if their bodies
           have been brutalized?
           Murdered?

           Dig.

STETKO   It was a war!
           I only did as I was told!

MEJRA   Such a good boy.
           What if you'd said no.

STETKO   They would have killed me.

MEJRA   Me or you.
           It comes to that.
           Me
           or you.

STETKO   War changes everything.
           Once you're in it —
           there are no choices.

MEJRA   Yes there are.
           Dig.

STETKO   Right.
                 "Dig."
                 Obey or die.
                 People will always obey rather than die.

MEJRA   Dig.

STETKO   Sure.
                 I'm not proud.
                 I'm no hero.
                 I'll dig.

                 He digs furiously.

                 I don't know about life.
                 I'm no great thinker.
                 What am I supposed to know that would change
                 things.

MEJRA   You should look at every woman as if she were your
                 daughter.

                 He stops.

                 Every woman
                 as if she were your daughter.

                 Dig.

STETKO   I can't.

MEJRA   You can
                 and you will.

STETKO   (*digs*) Okay.
                 Big deal.
                 Big f'ing deal.

                 I've hit something.

MEJRA   Keep digging.

STETKO   I think — (*looking closely, leaping out*) — it's a head!

MEJRA   Pull it out.

> *He looks frantic.*

Pull it out.

STETKO   I can't.

> *Long silence.*

> *STETKO walks into the grave and pulls at the corpse.*

Okay!
It's out!

MEJRA   Bring her here.

STETKO   Oh god —

> *He hauls it up and tosses the small corpse at her feet.*

MEJRA   Who is she?

STETKO   I don't know.

MEJRA   What was her name?

STETKO   I don't know!

> *Pause.*

MEJRA   Dig up the rest.

STETKO   Oh god!
Fucking hell —

       He stomps into the grave and digs.

       *MEJRA looks at the corpse and brushes dirt off
the decomposing skull.*

MEJRA   How old child?
You will not be forgotten.

       *STETKO tosses another decomposed body on the
ground. MEJRA goes to it and puts a finger
through a hole in the breast bone.*

Was it quick
or did you suffocate in the grave?

       *Another body, and another are unceremoniously
tossed out. MEJRA goes to one and bends low.*

Is it you?
(*kneeling*) Is it you?

       *She cradles the body in her arms, and rocks, and
begins to keen.*

       *STETKO climbs out and observes. When
MEJRA finally sees him she stops.*

       A long, long silence.

MEJRA   Come here.

       He does.

On your knees.

       He hesitates but obeys.

MEJRA   Hold her.

> *She offers the body to him.*

Hold her.

> *STETKO reluctantly holds out his arms to
> receive the corpse.*

Her name is Ana.
She was 19.
Young looking for her age.
She wanted to be a teacher — of philosophy.
She respected all religions.
She was brave and kind at once.

She had a thin line of black hair that ran up to her
navel.
And watery eyes
like a doe's.

She felt every person had dignity regardless of their
race.

She believed love was the answer.
Patience was the teacher.
Compassion was the mirror.
She would say, "I am the reflection of love and trust
and joy — all that you are
but haven't yet recognized
in yourself."

> *Silence.*

I felt her adjust her shoulder before she entered this
world. A world not yet ready for grace and beauty.

I never taught her about evil.
I thought I could protect her by hiding the truth.

Pause.

MEJRA   Give her back to me.

Pause.

*STETKO returns the corpse with as much grace
and reverence as he can. MEJRA stands. Silence.*

You can get up now.

He doesn't.

No longer "missing".

Get up.

STETKO   I can't.

MEJRA   You are going to dig up the rest
and then you have one more task.

You are going to tell the story of the missing ones.
The women and children you killed.
You are going to name them.
We are going to build a monument to the truth about
war.
We are going to let the mothers reclaim their
daughters.

STETKO   They'll kill me.
Then the truth will never be out.

MEJRA   The truth has a way of emerging.
Nothing can stop it
once it's started.
I may be gagged
my husband tortured
my house burned down
my land stolen

my children savaged
but the wind will speak my name
the waters will tell the fish
the fish will tell the hunter
"I am."
I am.

Blackout.

***

SCENE 8

*A monument of the dead bodies has been built.
The corpses have been seated, stacked in a circle,
looking out.*

*MEJRA is standing by the monument holding
the corpse of Ana in her arms. The basket with
the rabbit is near the monument. STETKO stands
centre stage holding one of the corpses in his
arms. He is uncertain and nervous.*

STETKO   Uh...

He looks at MEJRA.

MEJRA   Name them.

STETKO   I don't know who they are.

MEJRA   It's time.

STETKO   (*looking at the monument*) I don't know.
It's a blur.
You just did it.

MEJRA   "I". "I" did it.

STETKO   "I" just did it.
I...
killed them.

Silence.

STETKO   My girlfriend is missing.
                She has dark shoulder-length hair.
                She wears it in a pony-tail.

                She has green eyes.
                Her name
                is Ini.
                Ini Herak.

                     Pause.

MEJRA   Name all the girls you killed, Stetko.

STETKO   I didn't always ask their name.

                     Silence.

MEJRA   Describe them.

STETKO   I can't.

                     Pause.

MEJRA   Begin with the first.

STETKO   I don't know who she was.

MEJRA   What did she look like?

STETKO   ...She was older.
                Maybe 40.

                After I shot her I hid her body under a log.

MEJRA   Remember her.

                     He sets the corpse he is holding with the others.
                     It triggers a memory.

STETKO   She had had children. I saw stretch marks on her
belly.
She had a birth mark near her left shoulder — a purple
one shaped like a kidney bean.

Long silence.

I killed a girl named Mini. Fifteen.
She had a sun-burned face.
Luba, maybe 21.
And a young girl with reddish hair. Long. Down to
her waist.
A girl named Sara. She wore glasses. She was short
and chubby.
A married woman. She had a wedding ring with a tiny
diamond set into the band.
Monica. She had a gap between her two front teeth.

A girl with one brown eye and one green one.
Carol. I think she was pregnant.
Eva. She was a swimmer in training for the
Olympics.
A girl who said she was a waitress. She dyed her hair
blonde.
Dark roots were showing.
Misa. Sixteen.
Her older sister.
Twins. Thirteen. They looked identical.
A mother of 2 boys.
A girl with a scar on her right side.
An older woman who wore a copper bracelet on each
wrist.
A girl with a mole beside her left nipple.
A girl with pimples.
A girl with black lace-up boots.
A girl with big soft lips.

He has trouble continuing.

STETKO   Ana.
         Ana.

> *MEJRA, in a rage, rushes at STETKO with the
> shovel and strikes him on the back. He falls
> against the bodies and scrambles behind the
> monument. MEJRA pursues him and strikes him
> a single hard blow to the head. He falls still and
> silent, his feet extending beyond the bodies.*

> *Silence.*

> *MEJRA realizes she has killed him and is
> horrified. She fights back retching. She looks up
> and out and realizes her deed has been witnessed.
> She starts to flee, but can't. It's pointless. She's
> been seen and the deed too horrible to run from.
> She wants to scream but can't. She is like a
> caught animal. She runs back to STETKO.*

> *She decides to bury him, and after glancing
> around for a suitable spot, proceeds to drag him
> out by his feet. She begins to dig a hole when
> STETKO groans. She hears him and rushes to
> him, grabbing his head in her hands.*

Stetko?
Stetko!
Are you — ?!

> *She checks his breathing and unconsciously,
> ecstatic, hugs him to her chest.*

> *STETKO stirs. MEJRA, aware of her
> compromise, abruptly drops his head, stands up,
> apart, and resumes a hardness. STETKO sits up
> and rubs his head.*

> *Silence.*

STETKO   So, you're glad I'm alive, eh?

You're just like me, Mejra.
A murderer.
A slave and a dog.

MEJRA   Don't you compare us!

STETKO   "If you hate enough you can kill a people on
command?"
Who commanded you?
You think you're above it all, eh?
Once you got what you wanted from me then you
were going to do me in. Just like we do to prisoners.
You'd make a good soldier, Mejra.

MEJRA   I did it for my daughter!

STETKO   I had no daughter.
Only me.
Who are you to say who's more important?

MEJRA   I was doing it for love.

STETKO   That's what the soldiers say.
"Love for my country."

MEJRA   It's not the same!

STETKO   We all have our reasons, eh?
We all think we're right.

So, what's the answer
eh, Mejra?

MEJRA   She was innocent!

STETKO   War is no place for the innocent.

MEJRA   How dare you!

STETKO Going to kill me again?

> *MEJRA stops.*

> *Silence.*

Me or you.
Isn't that what you said?
Me
or you.

Who's it going to be?

Why don't you look at every man as if he were your son?

> *Silence.*

MEJRA Would you have died to save your girlfriend?

STETKO I don't know.
How do we ever know that?

MEJRA I would have cut my own throat to save Ana.
I would have endured rape by every last soldier.
They could have flayed me alive and dragged my wet body through the streets.

STETKO And you would kill for her too.

You can't win a war by dying for the enemy.

> *Pause.*

You willing to die for me, Mejra?

> *She is outraged at the idea. STETKO laughs at her.*

STETKO   So much for ideals, eh?

                It's easy to hate.
                Easy to kill once you feed that hate.

                Isn't that right, Mejra?

MEJRA   You make life unendurable.

STETKO   But we're here.
                You're here.
                I'm here.
                We made it.

MEJRA   Yes.
                There's no justice in this world.

STETKO   No.
                Dogs and slaves.

MEJRA   Dogs and slaves.

                Long silence.

                Get out of here.

                She tosses him the keys to his chains.

                You're free to go.

                STETKO does not go.

                Go.

                MEJRA turns to leave.

STETKO   Where will you go?

MEJRA   Back to the land.

STETKO   Can I go with you?

MEJRA   No.

STETKO   You need someone.

MEJRA   Not you.

STETKO   Who then?

              There is no one, is there?
              You're alone.

MEJRA   Go home to your family.

STETKO   They might take me back.

MEJRA   So go.

STETKO   Mejra?

                    No response.

              I'm sorry.
              I'm sorry for what I did.

                    Pause.

              Forgive me.

MEJRA   How?

STETKO   Pardon?

MEJRA   How can I forgive you?
              Show me.
              Show me how to forgive.
              I don't know how.

                    STETKO takes an uncertain step toward MEJRA.

STETKO   (*almost a whisper*) I'm sorry.

> *He unconsciously reaches out a finger to touch MEJRA's hand.*

Forgive me.

> *MEJRA unconsciously makes a movement in his direction.*

> *Slow fade on the monument of MEJRA and STETKO in a moment of possibilities.*

> *The End.*